Read About® Holidays

Valentine's Day

By Trudi Strain Trueit

Reading Consultant
Cecilia Minden-Cupp, PhD
Former Director of the Language and Literacy Program
Harvard Graduate School of Education
Cambridge, Massachusetts

Children's Press®
A Division of Scholastic Inc.
New York Toronto London Auckland Sydney
Mexico City New Delhi Hong Kong
Danbury, Connecticut

Designer: Herman Adler
Photo Researcher: Caroline Anderson
The photo on the cover shows two children sharing some
Valentine's Day candy.

Library of Congress Cataloging-in-Publication Data

Trueit, Trudi Strain.
  Valentine's Day / by Trudi Strain Trueit.
      p. cm. — (Rookie read-about holidays)
    ISBN-10: 0-531-12461-4 (lib. bdg.)   0-531-11819-3 (pbk.)
    ISBN-13: 978-0-531-12461-1 (lib. bdg.)   978-0-531-11819-1 (pbk.)
  1. Valentine's Day—Juvenile literature. I. Title. II. Series.
  GT4925.T78 2006
  394.2618—dc22   2006003960

CHILDREN'S PRESS, and ROOKIE READ-ABOUT®, and associated
logos are trademarks and/or registered trademarks of Scholastic Library
Publishing. SCHOLASTIC and associated logos are trademarks and/or
registered trademarks of Scholastic Inc.
5 6 7 8 9 10 R 16 15 14 13 12 11 10 09   62

Roses are red, violets are blue. On Valentine's Day, we say, "I love you!"

Valentine's Day began
in Rome, Italy. Long ago,
people living in Rome
could not marry.

The Roman ruler
Claudius II needed soldiers.
He thought married men
would not join his army.
So, Claudius said it was
against the law to marry.

A Roman soldier

5

IMP. C. M. AVR. CLAVDIVS. P. F. AVG. GERM. GOTTHICVS

CLAVDIVS, Gotthicus, Dalmata. Imperauit an II. mens.
.... sedente Dionysio, decessit an. Chr. CCLXX.

48

Claudius II

6

A priest named Valentine knew Claudius was wrong. Valentine performed weddings in secret. Claudius found out and threw Valentine in jail.

Valentine made friends
with the jailor's daughter.
He wrote notes to her.
He signed each one
"From your Valentine."

Valentine

A painting showing Saint Valentine (right)

Valentine was put to death on February 14 more than 1,700 years ago. He was killed because he broke the law. He eventually became known as Saint Valentine,

Years later, a French prisoner wrote poetry to his wife from his jail cell. People in Europe heard about the lonely prisoner. They remembered Saint Valentine, who brought couples together. People began calling the soldier's poems valentines.

The first valentines were sent from the inside of a French prison such as the one shown here.

February 2009

Sunday	Monday	Tuesday	Wednesday	Thursday	Friday	Saturday
1	2	3	4	5	6	7
8	9	10	11	12	13	14
15	16	17	18	19	20	21
22	23	24	25	26	27	28

The people of Europe soon
began celebrating February
14 by sending their own
valentines. They made
cards shaped like hearts.

Some signed their names. Others wrote "From your valentine," to keep the sender's name a secret.

The tradition of sending valentines each February 14 eventually spread to North America, Asia, and Australia.

An early valentine

A nineteenth-century valentine

Workers in factories made most valentines by the 1800s. These cards were decorated with silk, feathers, lace, and even gold!

Today we celebrate
Valentine's Day with cards
and gifts. People often
give one another candy
hearts or chocolates.

Ways to Celebrate

Some people give flowers to their loved ones. Red roses are a sign of true love.

Some children make valentines for their friends, classmates, and neighbors.

Making valentines

Other children visit hospitals or senior centers and hand out cards. Some take jars filled with candy hearts. Everyone guesses how many hearts are in the jar. Whoever is closest to the right number wins the candy.

Giving to others is a great way to cheer up people who are sick or lonely on Valentine's Day. It makes you feel good, too!

29

Words You Know

candy hearts

chocolates

Claudius II

giving

30

roses

soldiers

Saint Valentine

valentines

Index

About the Author

Trudi Strain Trueit is a former television news reporter and weather forecaster. She has written more than thirty fiction and nonfiction books for children. Ms. Trueit lives near Seattle, Washington, with her husband Bill.

Photo Credits

Photographs © 2007: akg-Images, London/Bibliothèque Nationale: 6, 30 bottom left; Alamy Images/foodfolio: 21, 30 top right; Art Resource, NY/Museum of London, London, UK/HIP: 18; Bridgeman Art Library International Ltd., London/New York: 13 (Musee de la Ville de Paris, Musee Carnavalet, Paris, France/Giraudon), 10 (Private Collection/Rafael Valls Gallery, London, UK); Corbis Images: 25, 31 bottom right (Lyn Hughes), 22, 30 bottom right (Royalty-Free), 26, 30 top left (Kirsten Soderlind); PhotoEdit/Michael Newman: 29; Superstock, Inc.: cover (age fotostock), 3, 31 top left (Rosemary Calvert), 17; The Art Archive/Picture Desk/Marc Charmet: 9, 31 bottom left; The Image Works/Museum of London/Topham: 5, 31 top right.